Father McBride's
TEEN CATECHISM

TEACHING GUIDE

Based on the Catechism of the Catholic Church

ALFRED McBRIDE, O. PRAEM.

Our Sunday Visitor Publishing Division
Our Sunday Visitor, Inc.
Huntington, Indiana 46750

Our Sunday Visitor Publishing Division
Our Sunday Visitor, Inc.
200 Noll Plaza
Huntington, Indiana 46750

ISBN: 0-87973-712-3

PRINTED IN THE UNITED STATES OF AMERICA

Cover design by Rebecca J. Heaston

712

ELEMENTS TO BE CONSIDERED IN THIS GUIDE

1. The goal of the *Teen Catechism*
2. The method used
3. Five things to remember about teenagers
4. Eight points to remember when teaching this course
5. Thirty-six lesson guides for the thirty-six lessons of this book

THE GOAL OF THE TEEN CATECHISM

The primary goal of the *Teen Catechism* is to help young people acquire a living, conscious and active faith in Jesus Christ by the light of instruction. Faith in Jesus is personal and communal. In the Apostles' Creed we say, "I believe." In the Nicene Creed we say, "We believe." Faith is a personal response to the saving work of Jesus. But our faith is in the context of the Church. Hence we always exercise our faith in a community of believers, as is clear from the Sunday liturgy, which is the highest expression of our faith on a weekly basis.

At the same time, our faith is a belief in the revealed truths given to us by God in scripture and proclaimed by the Church in her apostolic tradition and through her teaching office — the Magisterium of the popes and bishops. There is a "content" to our faith as found in the Bible, the creeds, the Catechism and the canons of the Ecumenical Councils of the Church. Theology, catechesis, homilies and evangelization help us understand and share this faith with others.

We celebrate and experience our faith in Father, Son and Holy Spirit in liturgy. We witness and practice our faith in obedience to the moral teachings of Jesus conserved and applied by the Magisterium throughout Church history.

All these elements about faith are found in the *Catechism of the Catholic Church*: Creed, the faith professed; Sacraments, the faith celebrated; Morality, the faith lived; Prayer, the faith deepened. The textbook that accompanies this guide illumines the basic teachings of the Catechism for a teenage audience.

THE METHOD USED

Every lesson follows this outline:
1. Story

2. Question
3. Wrong or inadequate answer
4. The right answer from the Catechism, along with some explanation
5. A further clarification of the teaching
6. A reflection on the truth taken from a saint, theologian, or other outstanding Catholic
7. "In My Life" — Series of questions to help teens apply truth to their lives
8. Prayer starter
9. Glossary (as necessary)

The heart of the method used in this book is a dialogue style that is designed to build upon the inquiring minds of young people and lead them to a discovery of the authentic teachings of Jesus. The false or inadequate answers to the proposed questions are drawn from positions currently held in the culture or by others who disagree with Church teachings. The responses taken from the Catechism have a double purpose: (1) They show the readers how to find specific Church teachings in the Catechism; (2) They create a familiarity with the Catechism and introduce them to a lifelong usage of it.

The reflections taken from other authors remind the teenagers of the "Theology of Abundance" so typical of Catholicism. For centuries we have had access to a rich inheritance of meditations on faith in Jesus. We have had access to a host of witnesses whose writings continue to share their love of Christ with us.

Since catechesis should never be merely an academic exercise, but relate to real life, the "In My Life" questions provide teens with the necessary challenge to take these teachings and see how they apply to their daily lives. The prayer is meant to be a "starter prayer" which could be used as the beginning of a meditation at the conclusion of the study section. Finally, the glossary specifies the identification of certain key terms in Church discourse, a vocabulary that enables us to communicate with each other at a commonly understood level.

Five Things to Remember About Teenagers

1. They are in midcourse between childhood and adulthood.

This transition naturally causes uncertainty, confusion about identity and shifting moods. One day they are up. The next day they are down. As the adult mentor, you must witness stability and strength of character so they can see how it works. At the same time, you should be sympathetic to their storm-tossed journey and walk with them as a gentle but firm guide. Matters may be complicated by the home life of the teens and also by neighborhoods that expose them to drugs and violence. Sensitivity to these contemporary pressures will increase your ability to help.

2. They are curious about everything.

They want to know the reasons for the faith they find within themselves and for the practices that faith demands. Encourage their questions and point them to the basic answers found in the teachings of Christ and the Church in the Catechism. Don't be afraid of their challenging questions, and have a sense of humor about their mischievous attempts to "corner the teacher."

3. They are idealistic — often to a fault.

But this idealism can be very helpful in motivating them to a strong faith and moral life. Encourage their idealism with examples of virtue found in the life of Jesus and the lives of saints and other great people. Too many people try to disillusion them with social realism. Of course they should know the bad and ugly facts of life. But they should also hear about the beauty and goodness and greatness of people. Facts are not enough. Possibilities are just as important. Nourish their dreams and hopes which can go beyond the sorrows and tragedies of everyday life. Develop their faith and hope and confidence.

4. They are emotional and romantic and personal.

Channel their feelings toward the love of God, others and self. The best way to discipline and control emotions is to direct them to actions which make the world a better place. Such an approach does not try to suppress feelings but rather to use emotion as energy placed at the service of love. The word emotion comes from the Latin *movere* which means "to move and motivate." There is a great deal of talk today about getting in touch with one's feelings. Generally, this is not the problem with teenagers who live very close to the ocean of feeling that accompanies the bursting life within them. A competent guide can do them a favor by marrying that sublime gift to action, which will make them highly motivated and do some good for the world in the meantime.

Because they are also both romantic and personal in their outlook, teens need to be approached on a personal level. The Catechism's teachings are generally crisp and abstract, the result of centuries of pruning away any excess in the expression of Christian truth. The statements are like polished rocks which have been buffed and sanded to near perfection. As a guide, you must translate these teachings into personal language with stories, examples, pictures and other concrete ways of making the teachings come alive. The

5

media says "Names make news." In catechesis the person makes news, above all the person of Jesus Christ.

5. They are becoming aware of their sexuality.

Much foolishness has been written about the "raging hormones" of teenagers, some of it to justify their being sexually active. Consequently, it is proposed, they should be given condoms and birth control pills to handle the problem. At the same time, there is no doubt that their newly found sexual feelings and development are real and exert a variety of pressures, anxieties and dilemmas upon them. This catechism is not a sex-education course, but we need to be aware of the sexual awareness of teenagers and the troubles as well as the joys this brings. Here adult wisdom is paramount. Be prepared to help the teens have a wholesome and grace-filled respect for sexuality.

The chapters on the sixth and ninth commandments in this book will provide some guidance. But your own faith and commitment to the Church's teachings on sex, marriage and chastity must be strong, giving evidence of your own continuing efforts to integrate the gift of sex into your whole humanity. These young people are going through a special process in their teenage years, but it is a lifelong journey as well.

EIGHT POINTS TO REMEMBER WHEN USING THE TEEN CATECHISM

Review the outline of each lesson found in the section on method (see pp. 3-4). With this outline fixed firmly in your mind, review the following eight teaching points.

1. Discuss the opening story.

Ask your teens if the story reminds them of similar ones in their own lives. Think about your own life and see if you have experiences you could share. Avoid saying, "When I was your age. . . ." That puts too much distance between yourself and them. The very fact you are an adult is distance enough. Sharing should have the tone of confidentiality, letting special people in on a secret. Naturally, your story should be prudent. There is little to be gained in sharing something you will regret having said later on, or a tale that the teens are not mature enough to hear. The story time is a community building moment as lives are knitted together in disclosures about each other's humanity.

Obviously the stories have another purpose as well, namely, to awaken the teenagers' interest in the catechetical teaching at hand. The surest to understand a truth is to approach it through the window of the imagination. First the picture, then the idea. We are not pure brains. We are a mix of body and mind, of flesh and soul. On this earth the physical must get its due as a servant of the spiritual. St. Thomas said, "There is nothing in the mind that was not first in the body." Stories are the easiest ways to employ the imagination at the service of truth, both human and divine.

2. Take time with the first answer to the question.

The first answer is always either wrong or inadequate. This answer is often drawn from popular misconceptions, misguided writers or myths promoted by the culture. Teens may already have similar confusing ideas. Or they may run into them in the future. The method employed here appeals to the questioning mind of young people. Questions are mind stretchers. They exercise the mind just as walking exercises the body. Someone has said that when the wind blows the trees exercise. That's what questions are designed to do in a teaching method. They introduce the spirit of inquiry, of search.

The use of the wrong answer-right answer approach is like a bad guy-good guy setup in a story. It creates interest, tension and release. Too many teachers begin with the answer before their students know what the question is. That is why the wag who heard that Jesus is the answer asked, "But what is the question?"

Introducing the question first along with an arguable answer gives them the "state of the question" and involves them in the search for the answer. This is a different approach from a teaching method that is all questions and no answers. It is actually quite easy to raise questions. That is why the proverb developed which says, "A fool can ask more questions than a wise man can answer."

3. Explain the Catechism's answer to the question.

It would be ideal if your teens each had a copy of the Catechism so that they could see the answers in the context of the Catechism itself. Show why the Catechism's answer is right and the first answer is wrong or inadequate. Always relate this to the development of the faith of the teenager. Be sure to personalize the truth, because their faith is not only in the content but also in the person of Jesus to whom the truth refers.

This is a revelation-based catechesis. God reveals. We respond personally, and communally in faith. The words of the Catechism trace themselves back to the Bible which narrates the religious experiences of people who met God. Hence we never stop at the sentences on the page. We go through them to meet God. They are like windows through which we perceive the sacred presence of Christ. Hence the words of the Catechism must make a journey from the eyes that read the page, the ears that hear the words, the mind that understands the truths — to the heart which touches God. This is a good catechetical process at its best.

In personalizing the Catechism's answers use scripture, the lives of the saints, inspiring events of Church history, heroic tales of outstanding Catholics to make the words come alive. Talk in visuals. Be specific, definite and concrete. Use images and pictures. They are as free as the air you breathe.

4. Use the third answer to clarify the truth.

When you deal with truth you must be like a long distance walker or a mountain hiker or a scuba diver. Every truth about Jesus is so deep, you will need a lifetime to find out all it means. Every truth about Christ *reveals* what you presently see and *conceals* what you have yet to behold. The study of divine truth is a never-ending story, an adventure in clarification and understanding. The word truth comes from a Greek term which means to raise the curtain. At the theater the curtain goes up to reveal the set and then it goes down, only to rise again on a new set. Truth is like that. It is a series of stage sets which draw you more and more into its treasures and involve you in the excitement of its story.

That is the purpose of the third answer in each lesson of this book. It is an exercise in clarifying truth. It's not the end of the story. The hiker has a big mountain to climb. The diver has unfathomable depths. The traveler has yet another city to see. This is only the beginning of the adventure of knowing Christ and understanding the truths he taught. The third answer is an invitation to keep on going, to love Jesus more deeply and to understand him more clearly.

5. Use the reflection for meditation time.

One of the beauties of the Church is that it is one of the oldest, continuing, vital communities and institutions in the world. The Church has been a major player in the lives of people for two thousand years. This incredible experience has produced a "wisdom community" whose record of wisdom has been lovingly preserved and whose meditations are more than dry manuscripts. The reflections of the saints, Church Fathers, mystics, and heroic Christians constitute a treasure of wisdom as alive today as when the words were first recorded.

The passages chosen for the reflection section of this book come from the Church's spiritual "bank" that has never closed. We can always make withdrawals and there is no charge for the transaction. Wisdom is free of charge. There is nothing casual or disposable about real wisdom. Its content is not like the newspaper, read today and tomorrow used to wrap dead fish.

Its lessons compare to a box of jewels. That is why we speak of "pearls" of wisdom.

The best way to use the reflection materials is for short meditation sessions. The busy work that you and your teens have engaged in with the question and its answers needs a silence break. Here is an excellent chance both to teach and practice meditation. Ask all present to close their eyes, quiet down and focus on the person of Jesus. Then you could either read the reflection slowly for them, or have them read it themselves.

After the reading, allow for five to ten minutes of silent meditation on the text. Perhaps they could underline a sentence that appealed to them. If so, invite them to repeat the words quietly, one at a time, with silence in between. The silence between the words draws them into the meditation. They may take each word and drop it into the silence of their hearts like a pebble dropped into a pool.

Normally this is not a time for explanations of the reflection, though you could respond privately if a teen wishes to ask about something. Here you are teaching them a lifetime habit of meditation, especially, if you do it thirty-six times for the thirty-six lessons. This is a simple way of giving them a depth approach to the Catechism.

6. Ask your young people to apply the message to their lives.

Above we noted that the Greek word for truth describes it in terms of a curtain and a stage set. But the Bible has another way of looking at truth. Scripture uses the word "emeth" for truth. Jesus said, "I have the truth." But he also declared, "I am the truth." In other words, truth is more than an idea in the mind. It must also be lived. Truth means fidelity as well as intellectual assent. The truth that is never lived dries out like a muscle that is never used.

Insight into truth comes from fidelity to what it asks. It is true that Jesus is our Savior. I can believe that in my mind. But if I do not accept his salvation by faith, the truth becomes unreal to me. If I do not beg every day that Christ's salvation be part of my continuing conversion to him, then the truth fades "like the last lingering smile of the cheshire cat."

Now you can see the purpose of the section in this book, "In My Life." Every chapter has three sets of questions to help teens practice biblical "emeth," the truth about Jesus that is both believed and practiced. This section is an exercise in loving fidelity to the truth and to the Christ to whom it points.

This is the most personal part of the lesson inasmuch as it challenges young people to make applications to their own lives and invites them to continue their faith conversion process. This is the moment in which they "create" the lesson by taking the raw material of their lives and by confronting the truths about Jesus, the truths of Jesus, the person of Jesus.

This encounter can be very productive for them because it induces a moment of self-knowledge and opens them to possibilities which they had not yet seen. They can move from fact to possibility, enlarge their spiritual horizons and nail down pursuits of virtue through the resolutions they make.

7. It's time for shared prayer.

Every lesson contains a prayer. Consider it a "prayer starter." Your teen has already studied and meditated on the lesson. The meditative time was personal. This prayer time should be communal. Teens need to see that Catholicism is communal and collaborative. Begin by saying the prayer together. Then have a brief period of silence. Invite your teens to offer their personal prayers.

8. Master the glossary.

From the viewpoint of mastery of the material, the assimilation of the glossary is the simplest way to do it. As we try to restore a modicum of religious literacy, the acquisition of a common vocabulary with meanings provided by the Catechism is essential. This is only the beginning of such a procedure.

An accepted vocabulary is far from being the whole story, but it is a basis from which to start. The other seven points mentioned above outline the complex riches to which we expose the student of the Catechism. Any focus on code words must be integrated into all the other matters which have been covered.

Every educational discipline has its code words which are readily understandable by the others in the field. Catechesis, insofar as it is an educational discipline, participates in this common endeavor. This never excludes spontaneity of expression so long as the extensions are consistent with the fundamental teachings of the Catechism. Nor does this interfere with other dimensions of faith development at the level of prayer, meditation, worship and theology.

Summary

These eight teaching points should be integrated into one vision of how to use this book. The advice needs to be related to the understanding of the goal of the text, the method being used and the comments about the lives of teenagers today. Most of the material has been presented here in a checklist form to make it easier for you to see each piece of the puzzle to give you a way of seeing how comprehensive your own approach is.

Thirty-six Lesson Guides for the Thirty-six Chapters of the Book

You will next find some brief guidance for each of the thirty-six lessons in this book. Each lesson guide contains the following material:

Goal of the Lesson
Suggested Opening *Hymn*
Suggested *Scripture Reading*
Comments
The Result
What Should We Do?
One *Resource*

This outline is meant to help you get a handle on the substance of each lesson. The material in *Comments* is not meant to be exhaustive in any sense of the word. The *Comments* are stimulants for your own thoughts and imagination. Much the same can be said of the sections *The Result and What Should We Do?*

I have stayed with this outline for the sake of consistency, but you will have your own approaches to teaching. Basically, I am just offering idea starters. You may want and need more than is offered here, or this may be just right for you. Stay loose and let the gifts of the Spirit help you see what is the best way to enhance the faith life of your teens.

Chapter 1

The Desire for God Is Written on Our Hearts

Goal: To explain why it is valid to say that humans are basically religious and that God can be known from reason and the experience of a capacity for God.

Hymn: "How Great Thou Art" (*Breaking Bread* hymnal, 405)

Scripture Reading: Romans 1:19-20

Comments:

1. The communications explosion has so overwhelmed modern awareness with a message that is materialistic and secular that people today find it difficult to experience their basically religious nature.

2. At a deeper level, the impact of the eighteenth-century Enlightenment philosophy weakened our capacity to transcend ourselves and so come to a knowledge of God through reason or from a sense of our capacity for God.

3. At an even deeper side of ourselves, the outcome of original sin darkens our minds, weakens our wills and causes disorder in our emotions and passions.

The Result: We often think of ourselves in purely secular terms and have forgotten our capacity for God.

What Should We Do?

A. Recognize the secular character of the culture.
B. Point out the numerous signs of a hunger for God.
C. Discuss experiences that have drawn people to God.

Resource: *Handbook of Christian Apologetics*, Peter Kreeft and Ronald Tacelli, Intervarsity Press, Downers Grove, IL, 1994.

Chapter 2

REVELATION:
GOD CALLS US TO LOVE AND TO COMMUNION

Goal: To show we need revelation to understand fully what it means to relate to God.

Hymn: "Holy, Holy, Holy, Lord God Almighty" (*Worship, Third Edition*, 485)

Scripture Reading: Isaiah 6:1-13

Comments:

1. Human reason and our capacity for God can tell us there is a God. Original sin and other factors often make this very difficult. In his love, God realized our weakness and revealed himself to us.

2. Even if reason can know God, this knowledge is minimal. We need to know how to relate to God. In revelation God tells us how to do it and gives us the power to accomplish this communion.

3. We need revelation to know about how God planned to save us from our sin through Jesus Christ. Revelation also tells us truths such as Trinity, Incarnation, Salvation, Mary's Role, Grace, Church Sacraments, Last Things, etc.

The Result: In revelation God tells us how much he loves us. He gives us the gift of faith to respond.

What Should We Do?

A. Make many acts of faith and thanks for our salvation.
B. Make many acts of love for God to set our souls on fire.
C. Praise God constantly for the abundance of his blessings.

Resource: *The Catholic Vision*, Edward D. O'Connor, C.S.C., Our Sunday Visitor, Huntington, IN, 1992.

Chapter 3

Faith: My Response to God's Revelation

Goal: To become aware of the importance of faith as the proper response to God's revelation.

Hymn: "We Walk By Faith" (*Gather, Second Edition*, 414)

Scripture Reading: Hebrews 11:1-3

Comments:

1. Faith is a gift from God. We cannot reason to faith by steps of logic, though reason can prepare the receptivity of our hearts to be open to the gift.

2. Faith is personal, so we say, "I" believe in God. Faith is also communal, so we say, "We" believe in God. Because faith is personal, I am loved by God and can return love. Because faith is communal, I always believe in community with the Church.

3. Faith also is belief in truths of revelation. This is the "content" of our faith. These truths take a lifetime to penetrate by prayer and meditation.

The Result: We see that our religion is a dialogue of revelation and faith, God's call and my response. Faith is a gift, a relationship and belief in the truths (the content) of revelation.

What Should We Do?

A. Pray many times, "I believe, Lord. Help my unbelief."
B. Gain strength for faith at community worship.
C. Study the truths of revelation with ever deeper faith.

Resource: *Essentials of the Faith*, Alfred McBride, O.Praem., Our Sunday Visitor, Huntington, IN, 1994.

Chapter 4

REVELATION IS COMMUNICATED THROUGH TRADITION AND SCRIPTURE

Goal: To show that God's revelation has been recorded in scripture, transmitted through apostolic tradition.

Hymn: "Lord, You Give the Great Commission" (*Worship, Third Edition*, 470)

Scripture Reading: Matthew 28:16-20

Comments:

1. The religious experience of God's people — an event of revelation and faith response — in both the Old and New Testaments was recorded in scripture and passed on by apostolic tradition.

2. Revelation, therefore, comes to us in scripture and through apostolic tradition. Jesus gave the apostles authority to teach and conserve the truths of revelation. The apostles passed this power on to their successors, the popes and bishops.

3. It is the Magisterium of popes and bishops who have received the gift of the Spirit to determine what is truly the teaching of revelation and the proper understanding thereof.

The Result: God not only entered into a relation with us, but also established the permanent means whereby his revelation could be authentically transmitted.

What Should We Do?

A. Recognize revelation in scripture and apostolic tradition.
B. Appreciate the role of the Magisterium.
C. Experience the assurance this gives our faith.

Resource: *The Oxford Dictionary of the Popes*, J.N.D. Kelly, Oxford University Press, 1986.

Chapter 5

I Believe in God the Father Almighty

Goal:	To show that God is one, personal, loving — a Father who created us.
Hymn:	"Father, We Thank Thee, Who Hast Planted" (*Worship, Third Edition*, 558)

Scripture Reading: John 14:5-9

Comments:

1. When Moses met God at the burning bush, he asked the Lord's name. God replied with personal terms, "I Am." Moses learned that God was not the sun, the moon, the stars, a force, but rather a person who loved him and his people.

2. Scripture often speaks of God as Father. Jesus called God Father forty-five times. God is the divine Father of the divine Son. Our Father makes us in his image. Our Father shares his divine life and love with us. We become images of God simply by being born. We become adopted sons and daughters of God by being born again in baptism.

3. God is also the creator of the world and all it contains, especially human beings, as is clear from the creation stories in Genesis 1-3.

The Result:	Our God is loving, personal, fatherly, creative and providential. God wants to save us from sin.

What Should We Do?

A. Approach God as one who is personal and loving.
B. Meditate on Jesus to see what the Father is like.
C. Pray the Our Father as the principal prayer of our faith.

Resource:	*Rich in Mercy* (*Dives in Misericordia*), Encyclical of Pope John Paul II, Nov. 30, 1980.

Chapter 6

THE HOLY TRINITY:
GLORY TO THE FATHER, SON AND SPIRIT

Goal: To meditate on the central mystery of the Christian faith that God is Trinity, one God in three divine persons.

Hymn: "Praise God From Whom All Blessings Flow" (*Breaking Bread* hymnal, 369)

Scripture Reading: John 16:1-11

Comments:

1. Revelation teaches us that God is Father, Son and Holy Spirit. God is One. God is a unity in three persons.

2. The Councils of Nicaea, First Constantinople, Ephesus and Chalcedon described this mystery in terms of nature and person. God is three persons possessing one divine nature. The one-ness is in the divine nature. The three-ness is in the three divine persons.

3. The Father gives us life and providentially sustains us. The Son has redeemed us and continues to save us. The Holy Spirit sanctifies us and continues to make us ever holier.

The Result: We are the beneficiaries of Trinitarian love that creates, saves and sanctifies us in our lifelong conversion process.

What Should We Do?

A. Make the Sign of the Cross with an awareness of Trinity.
B. Be open to the unique blessing from each divine person.
C. Pray often: Glory to the Father, Son and Holy Spirit.

Resource: *Augustine* (Chapter 8 on the Trinity), Henry Chadwick, Oxford University Press, 1986.

Chapter 7

THE CREATION, FIRE AND SNOW, BLESS THE LORD

Goal: To show that God, Father, Son and Spirit created the world and continues to look after it and all living beings.

Hymn: "Nature's Praise" (*Gather* hymnal, 199)

Scripture Reading: Daniel 3:57-88

Comments:

1. Since the Enlightenment, which said God was like a clockmaker who started the world and then left it to us, there has been a progressive forgetfulness of the real role of God.

2. God is more than a mechanic who started the world. God is the Creator of the world and all living beings and God continues to keep everything in existence. This is called God's providence.

3. But God is more than a divine fixer that keeps us going. God is a divine lover who has a plan to save us from all that oppresses us, above all from sin. God is involved with us. We discover the divine plan in revelation and are asked to surrender with faith and confidence to the watchful plan of God as it occurs in history through the saving work of Christ.

The Result: We must overcome the modern prejudice that acts as though it does not matter that God is the origin of creation and our destiny.

What Should We Do?

A. Reaffirm our faith in God as creator, sustainer, redeemer.
B. Remember that it is in God we live, move, have our being.
C. Be a responsible steward of the creation God gave us.

Resource: Listen to the music and text of Haydn's "Creation."

Chapter 8

MADE IN THE IMAGE OF GOD

Goal: To reaffirm our faith in ourselves as images of God and to understand what that means.

Hymn: "Amazing Grace" (*Worship, Third Edition*, 583)

Scripture Reading: Genesis 1:27-28; 2:15-25

Comments:

1. Since the time of Darwin and the various positions on evolution, there has been an increasing forgetfulness about the role of God in the creation of man and woman. God is the creator, sustainer and redeemer of man and woman.

2. *The Church in the Modern World* (*Gaudium et Spes*), 2-22, from the documents of the Second Vatican Council, speaks of the human being as the center and crown of creation and an image of God who can know the truth, will the good, act freely in reference to truth and goodness, is aware of the divine source of his human dignity and is a communal person.

3. Therefore, *being* an image of God is not something passive, but a dynamic reality calling us *to act* as images of God.

The Result: In a culture where humans are degraded by violence, drink, drugs, we are called to uphold the sacredness of the person and energetically defend human dignity.

What Should We Do?

A. Take up the cause of human importance as image of God.

B. Resist all forms of destruction of human dignity.

C. See how Jesus reveals to us what it means to be human.

Resource: *The Abolition of Man*, C. S. Lewis, Colier, NY, 1947.

Chapter 9

ORIGINAL SIN — PARADISE LOST

Goal:　　　　　To reflect on the basic truth about human nature, that it has been radically flawed by original sin.

Hymn:　　　　　"Come to the Water" (*Gather, Second Edition*, 349)

Scripture Reading: Romans 5:17-21

Comments:

1. There are three views of human nature. The pessimistic stance says we are essentially bad. The optimistic approach claims we are essentially good. The realistic position states we are good but radically flawed.

2. Original sin is a teaching that follows the realistic view. We are good but basically flawed. However, by Christ's work we have been radically redeemed, provided we accept his grace in faith and baptism and active membership in the Church.

3. The effects of original sin remain after baptism. Hence we need lifelong conversion through prayer, worship, repentance and a commitment to the moral life.

The Result:　　The culture sees us either as devils or angels. We are neither. We are people in the process of being saved.

What Should We Do?

　　A. Acquire a realistic view of human nature.
　　B. Recognize original sin and its effects.
　　C. Praise Christ for the gift of salvation.

Resource:　　　*Essentials of the Faith* (Chapter 10 on Original Sin), Alfred McBride, O.Praem., Our Sunday Visitor, Huntington, IN, 1994.

Chapter 10

WE HAVE HEARD THE QUESTION:
JESUS IS THE ANSWER

Goal: To show that Jesus Christ, the Son of God and Son of Mary came to earth to save us from our sinfulness.

Hymn: "To Jesus Christ, Our Sovereign King" (*Worship, Third Edition*, 497)

Scripture Reading: I Peter 2:21-24

Comments:

1. Secular culture likes to reduce Jesus to just another man, a great one indeed, but nothing more than a man. He was thus admired as a fine moral teacher, one among many, pretty much on the same par as Mohammed, Buddha and Krishna.

2. We believe that Jesus is the Son of God, Son of Mary and savior of the world. In one sense, he is like us in all things except sin. But on the other hand, Jesus is absolutely unique. There is no one else like him, because no other person was both divine and human and a savior as well.

3. With St. Peter we profess that regarding Jesus, "There is no other name under heaven given among men by which we must be saved" (Acts 4:12).

The Result: We part company from those who would reduce Jesus to the purely human level. We adore and praise him as our savior.

What Should We Do?

A. Believe in the real Jesus Christ. Don't settle for less.
B. Increase our faith and devotion to Jesus.
C. Share our faith in Christ with others.

Resource: *Life of Christ*, Fulton Sheen, Doubleday, 1977.

Chapter 11

Blessed Be Jesus Christ, True God and True Man

Goal: To strengthen a comprehensive faith in the whole Jesus, both God and man.

Hymn: "Jesu, Joy of Our Desiring" (*Breaking Bread* hymnal, 320)

Scripture Reading: Colossians 1:15-20

Comments:

1. Scripture contains the revelation of the Trinity. The Old Testament reveals the Father. The Gospels show us the Son of God and Son of Mary. The Acts and Epistles disclose the person and acts of the Holy Spirit.

2. This is the context for studying the divinity and humanity of Jesus. The first four Councils of the Church addressed challenges to the traditional teaching about the Trinity and the full identity of Jesus Christ. They concluded that in Jesus Christ there was one divine person and two natures.

3. Therefore, the acts of Jesus' life are mysteries which invite our contemplation and communicate graces to us.

The Result: Jesus is the answer to human questions about death, future life, suffering and the meaning of life. He reveals our humanity to us.

What Should We Do?

A. Draw strength from communion with Christ's mysteries.
B. See Jesus as a model and teacher, but also a savior.
C. Let Jesus be our best friend.

Resource: *To Look on Christ: Exercises in Faith, Hope & Love*, Joseph Cardinal Ratzinger, Crossroad, NY, 1991.

Chapter 12

THE WONDROUS CROSS — THE EASTER GARDEN

Goal: To show that the death and resurrection of Jesus form one mystery of salvation.

Hymn: "Now the Green Blade Rises" (*Breaking Bread* hymnal, 192)

Scripture Reading: Philippians 2:5-11

Comments:

1. While the paschal mystery is one saving action of Jesus, there is a tendency to emphasize either the cross or the resurrection. We must include both as they belong together.

2. Christ's death is a death to sin. His resurrection is a rising to new life. The removal of our sins opens us to a new life in Christ. In our baptism we live this mystery by dying to sin and rising to a life of grace.

3. Christ's resurrection was not tacked on to the passion like a pleasant addition. The risen Jesus wears the marks of the passion. God is the author of this drama which is not a tragedy, but an event with a true happy ending.

The Result: It is above all in the paschal mystery that our salvation was achieved. Christ's cross and glory belong together.

What Should We Do?

A. Take the cross. Deny ourselves. Follow Jesus.

B. Live the resurrection by becoming a person of hope.

C. Invite others to become disciples of Jesus.

Resource: *Images of Jesus*, Alfred McBride, O.Praem., St. Anthony Messenger Press, Cincinnati, 1993.

Chapter 13

Breathe on Me, Breath of God

Goal: To contemplate the action of the Holy Spirit in the life of each Christian and in the Church.

Hymn: "Come, Holy Ghost" (*Worship, Third Edition*, 482)

Scripture Reading: Acts 2:1-4;42-47

Comments:

1. The Holy Spirit is the third person of the Blessed Trinity, sent to manifest the Church at Pentecost and to abide with the Church that its mission of salvation and kingdom building may be effective.

2. The Holy Spirit brings us gifts of wisdom, knowledge, understanding, courage, counsel, piety and fear of the Lord. The Spirit's greatest gift is love, which puts force and motivation into our life of virtue.

3. The Holy Spirit sanctifies us by moving us away from our sinfulness and moving us toward God. The Spirit's process of sanctification affects us throughout our lives as we grow deeper in our faith, hope and love of God, others and self.

The Result: In baptism, confirmation and the other sacraments, the Spirit incorporates us into the Church and makes us his temples.

What Should We Do?

A. Pray that the Spirit make us his temples from head to toe.
B. Turn to the Spirit to be filled with joy, love and peace.
C. Meditate on the Spirit's impact on the Church.

Resource: *Lord and Giver of Life (Dominum et Vivificantem)*, Encyclical of John Paul II, 1986.

Chapter 14

THE CHURCH IS THE BODY OF CHRIST

Goal: To grasp the essentials about the Church as Body of Christ, People of God, Temple of the Spirit and Sacrament of Salvation and the Kingdom.

Hymn: "The Church's One Foundation" (*Breaking Bread* hymnal, 404)

Scripture Reading: John 15:1-10

Comments:

1. The Church as a mystery of God: This emphasizes the supernatural aspect of the Church as founded by God, instituted by Christ and maintained by the Holy Spirit.

2. We are so accustomed to looking at the visible Church that we may forget its invisible and most sacred character as the Body of Christ and Temple of the Holy Spirit. It is also made up of the People of God — an expression that focuses on God calling us to membership in the Church.

3. At the same time the Church is a visible institution that serves us as Mother and Teacher and a conscience for the world.

The Result: The Church is the Sacrament of Salvation and the Kingdom, effectively making these gifts of Christ available to us and the world.

What Should We Do?

A. Love the Church as our Mother and Teacher.
B. Practice unity, holiness, catholicity, apostolicity.
C. Evangelize others into communion with the Church.

Resource: *Constitution on the Church* (*Lumen Gentium*), from the documents of the Second Vatican Council.

Chapter 15

Holy Mary, Mother of God, Pray for Us

Goal: To develop a doctrinally sound devotion to and appreciation of Mary the Mother of God.

Hymn: "My Soul Rejoices" (*Breaking Bread* hymnal, 442)

Scripture Reading: Luke 1:46-55

Comments:

1. At the Annunciation, Mary of Nazareth responded to God's call to be the mother of his Son with faith, obedience and humility. Throughout her life she stood as the model of faith for us all. Against those who would deny it, the Council of Ephesus declared Mary to be the *Theotokos* — Mother of God.

2. Mary is our sterling example of prayer. At Nazareth her prayer led her to be the mother of the incarnate Jesus. At Pentecost her prayer led the apostles and disciples, and she became the mother of the Mystical Body of Christ.

3. Mary intercedes for us in heaven as she did on earth when at Cana she asked Jesus to help the embarrassed couple.

The Result: Mary is the Queen of angels and saints, of heaven and earth and Mother of God. All her gifts proceed from her relation to Jesus.

What Should We Do?

A. Develop a lifelong, prayerful devotion to Mary.
B. Ask Mary to bring us closer to Jesus.
C. Relate to Mary as our holy Mother.

Resource: Read chapter 8, "Our Lady," in the *Constitution on the Church* (*Lumen Gentium*), 52-68, from the documents of the Second Vatican Council.

Chapter 16

DEATH AND JUDGMENT

Goal: To strengthen our faith in the last things — death, judgment, heaven, purgatory and hell.

Hymn: "We Shall Rise Again" (*Gather, Second Edition*, 558)

Scripture Reading: Matthew 25:31-46

Comments:

1. Secular culture concentrates on this life only. Psychology notes that people even deny death, meaning they don't want to think about it. The Church, on the other hand looks honestly at the fact of death and summons us to look at what happens after death: judgment, heaven, hell, purgatory, heaven.

2. We should spend quality time while we are alive, properly preparing for our death and already beginning to live eternal life here through sacramental celebration and a life of virtue.

3. While fear of hell may deter us from sin, the love of God is a better motivation.

The Result: Forgetfulness of our personal deaths and ignoring future life is a bad idea. Faith realism urges us to face reality.

What Should We Do?

A. Live each day as though it were our last one on earth.
B. Prepare for death and future life with love and hope.
C. Leave the world a legacy of charity, justice and mercy.

Resource: *Making Sense Out of Suffering*, Peter Kreeft, Servant Publications, Ann Arbor, 1986.

Chapter 17

THE CELEBRATION OF THE CHRISTIAN MYSTERIES

Goal: To show that the liturgy of the Church is an action of the Father, Son and Spirit, bringing us salvation and the kingdom of love, justice and mercy.

Hymn: "Praise, My Soul, the King of Heaven" (*Worship, Third Edition*, 530)

Scripture Reading: Revelation 4:1-11

Comments:

1. Liturgy is always the action of the Holy Trinity pouring out abundant blessings on the worshippers who gather in faith to praise God and receive the gifts of salvation and the kingdom.

2. In the liturgical gathering the whole assembly is a worshipping community — each member, priest and people, acting according to his or her function. The liturgy involves signs and symbols that relate to creation and the history of salvation.

3. The liturgy of the Word is an integral part of the sacramental celebration. Songs and music are closely connected to the liturgical celebration. Sunday is its most important day.

The Result: By the will of God and the action of the Trinity, the liturgy affords us the experience of praising God and receiving the gifts of salvation.

What Should We Do?

A. Become regular active participants in the liturgy.
B. Realize both God's action and our response at liturgy.
C. Develop a sense of awe and reverence proper to liturgy.

Resource: *St. Joseph Sunday Missal*, Catholic Book Publishers, New York.

Chapter 18

Born Again in Water and the Spirit

Goal: To demonstrate that baptism and confirmation are the first two of the three sacraments of initiation.

Hymn: "Baptized in Water" (*Worship, Third Edition*, 720)

Scripture Reading: John 3:16

Comments:

1. Sacraments are effective signs, instituted by Jesus, entrusted to the Church for the purpose of giving us a share in divine life. They are signs that point to, contain and produce the reality they signify.

2. Baptism is the real "born again" experience. Our first birth is physical from the womb of our mothers. Our second birth is spiritual, from the womb of the font of Mother Church.

3. Confirmation perfects baptismal grace. It is the sacrament that gives us the Holy Spirit in a more perfect manner and roots us more deeply in the life of Jesus.

The Result: Baptism literally gives us a new start in life, while confirmation perfects that initiation and endows us with the courage to be Christian.

What Should We Do?

A. Praise God for our baptism and live a new life in Christ.
B. Renew our baptismal promises every Sunday.
C. Become newly aware of our confirmation responsibilities.

Resource: *The Rites of the Catholic Church*, Volume I, Chapter on Baptism-Confirmation, Liturgical Press, Collegeville, MN, 1983.

Chapter 19

WE REMEMBER HOW YOU LOVED US

Goal: To dwell with faith on the Holy Eucharist as the summit and source of the Christian life.

Hymn: "I Am the Bread of Life" (*Breaking Bread* hymnal, 428)

Scripture Reading: John 6:22-71

Comments:

1. The tremendous wealth of the Eucharist is expressed in the different names we give it. Read the Catechism (1328-32) for ten major names given to the Eucharist — such as Sacrifice of the Mass, Breaking of Bread, Divine Liturgy, the Lord's Supper, etc.

2. The celebration of the Eucharist makes present Christ's work of salvation in the mysteries of his life, death, resurrection, ascension and coming again in glory. We actively participate according to our function with faith, hope, love.

3. The Liturgy of the Hours extends the Eucharistic celebration throughout the day and night. Hence altar, choir and tabernacle form an interconnected triad of graces for us.

The Result: The heart of Catholic life is the Mass whose riches are supplemented by the Liturgy of the Hours and devotion to the Real Presence.

What Should We Do?

A. Make the Mass a non-negotiable center of our lives.
B. Prepare for each Sunday liturgy using our Missal.
C. Visit the tabernacle frequently. Pray the Hours.

Resource: *The Hidden Manna: A Theology of the Eucharist*, James T. O'Connor, Ignatius, San Francisco, 1988.

Chapter 20

The Healing Touch of Christ

Goal: To understand how Jesus wants to heal us spiritually, morally and physically through the sacraments of healing.

Hymn: "I Heard the Voice of Jesus Say" (*Worship, Third Edition*, 607)

Scripture Reading: John 20:19-23; James 5:14-15

Comments:

1. In his Gospel ministry, Jesus healed the sick and forgave sins. In his risen life, Jesus continues this healing ministry through the sacraments of reconciliation and anointing.

2. Baptism gives our souls a "clean slate," but unfortunately we sin again. By his ministry of compassion, through the ministry of the priest, Jesus forgives our sins if we come to the sacrament of reconciliation with a penitent heart and confession of sins. This reunites us to Jesus and the Church.

3. In grave illness caused either by disease or old age, Jesus anoints us through the priest and prepares us for eternal life.

The Result: Jesus knows our weakness and is prepared to heal us and bring us home again. Our faith urges us to reconciliation and anointing.

What Should We Do?

A. Remember that our journey is a continual conversion.
B. Never be afraid to seek the mercy of Christ.
C. Practice forgiving others as we have been forgiven.

Resource: *Apostolic Constitution on Penance* (*Paenitemini*), Pope Paul VI, 1966 (Found in Flannery's *Vatican Council II*, Vol. 2, Costello, Northport, NY).

Chapter 21

THE SACRED ACTS OF MARRIAGE

Goal: To probe the riches of the sacrament of marriage and the importance of family values.

Hymn: "We Have Been Told" (*Gather, Second Edition*, 501)

Scripture Reading: Exodus 19:3-6; Ephesians 5:21-33

Comments:

1. The perilous state of the institution of marriage in our present culture needs more than ever the Church's teaching on the sacrament of marriage. The goals of marriage as an unbreakable bond of the unitive (love) and procreative (open to children) must be restated and encouraged.

2. Couples should be made aware of the role of covenant, the graces available from Christ and intrinsic link between the spiritual and physical aspects of marriage.

3. Openness to children should be augmented by a positive presentation of Natural Family Planning and the rich teachings of Pope Paul VI in *Humanae Vitae*.

The Result: The stability of our society and civilization is at risk unless strong marriages become the norm of our society once again.

What Should We Do?

A. Spouses should resolve to be promise keepers.
B. Spouses should be ready to work through their problems.
C. Spouses should rely strongly on faith and prayer.

Resource: *The Christian Family in the Modern World* (*Familiaris Consortio*), Pope John Paul II, 1981 (Flannery, Vatican Council II, Vol. 2).

Chapter 22

THE BEAUTY OF THE CATHOLIC PRIESTHOOD

Goal: To explore the Church's teaching on the ordained priesthood.

Hymn: "Go Up to the Altar of God" (James Chepponis, choral piece, G.I.A. Publications)

Scripture Reading: John 17:1-19

Comments:

1. At the Last Supper, Jesus brought the apostles into the ordained priesthood when he said to the Father, "Consecrate them in the truth" and when he said to them, "Do this in memory of me."

2. Ordained priesthood differs essentially from the baptized priesthood of the faithful. Baptized priesthood originates in Jesus as model of holiness and is directed to the sanctification of the world. Ordained priesthood originates in Jesus as head of the Church and is directed to the sanctification of the faithful.

3. A good priest will always center his life on the Eucharist whose mystery he celebrates and whose meaning he should witness.

The Result: The priest occupies a central role of bridge builder in the Church because of his acting in the person of Christ.

What Should We Do?

A. Priests should be loving shepherds of God's people.

B. Parents should foster priestly vocations.

C. Priests and people need to build communion.

Resource: *Priesthood*, Patrick Dunn, Alba House, NY, 1990.

Chapter 23

Building Blocks for the Catholic Moral Life

Goal: To outline the foundational truths upon which the Catholic moral life is built.

Hymn: "Take Up Your Cross" (*Breaking Bread* hymnal, 127)

Scripture Reading: Matthew, chapters 5-7

Comments:

1. All Christian morality begins with a covenant between God and the person within the context of the Church. Christ's laws of love of God, neighbor and self succinctly capture what covenant means.

2. A second building block is happiness as a motive for being moral. That is the purpose of Christ's eight beatitudes at the beginning of his great morality talk, the Sermon on the Mount. Happiness is the best reason to be right and good.

3. Other building blocks include: the life of virtue, the graces of the Spirit, the understanding of sin, the formation of conscience (by the natural law, the ten commandments, the teachings of Christ and the Church). These four elements form and inform our consciences. A life of virtue makes this a reality.

The Result: All study and behavior should result in a good person who does the right thing.

What Should We Do?

A. Train our consciences properly and practice virtue.

B. Keep covenant with Christ and ask the Spirit's graces.

C. Always take responsibility for our actions.

Resource: *Splendor of Truth* (*Veritatis Splendor*), John Paul II, 1993.

My Soul Thirsts for the Living God — The First Commandment

Goal: To see the meaning of the first commandment as a call to faith in a real God and the rejection of false gods.

Hymn: "Let All Mortal Flesh Keep Silence" (*Worship, Third Edition, 523*)

Scripture Reading: Psalm 139:1-24

Comments:

1. The real God is the God of the Bible. From revelation we know the story of God because God has told us who he is. Nonetheless, human pride will go on making false gods out of money, sex, power, food, transient good looks, etc. The superstars of popular culture and the personality cults of politicians are samples of false gods.

2. The real God is someone who loves us and has devised a plan to save us from our foolishness and selfishness. This divine plan was realized in Christ and is the only way to true joy.

3. Our response to the real God is faith that contains obedience, humility and love.

The Result: The real God formed a covenant people first with Israel and then with Christianity. The Church nourishes our faith in a real God.

What Should We Do?

A. Examine our lives and see how real our faith is.
B. Counter the culture's false gods with the true God.
C. Praise the true God from whom all blessings flow.

Resource: *Your God Is Too Small*, J.B. Phillips, Macmillan, NY, 1964.

Chapter 25

Rediscover the Sacred —
The Second Commandment

Goal: To unlock the key to the second commandment which is reverence and awe for the sacredness of God and life.

Hymn: "The Stars Declare His Glory" (*Gather, Second Edition*, 344)

Scripture Reading: Psalm 19: 1-15

Comments:

1. The prevalence of secularity in our culture proves not only that "the world is too much with us" but also that the sense of the sacred is in short supply. The second commandment urges us to search for the sacred in our world and our lives.

2. The coarseness of modern entertainment is a sign of the loss of fundamental reverence for persons. This leads to a disrespect for public institutions and finishes up in the despising of God. Only the restoration of the sacred will counter this.

3. The second commandment's focus on the sacred is the reason for clean language, a caring treatment of persons and the conservation of beauty in our lives.

The Result: The revival of a neo-pagan society is undoing centuries of Christian efforts to civilize society.

What Should We Do?

A. Resolve to restore reverence for persons and God.
B. Clean up language in films and books and conversation.
C. Never use God's name to justify injustices.

Resource: *The Mystery We Proclaim*, Francis Kelly, Our Sunday Visitor, Huntington, IN, 1993.

Chapter 26

WORTHY IS THE LAMB TO RECEIVE HONOR, GLORY AND BLESSING — THE THIRD COMMANDMENT

Goal: To understand the importance of the sabbath and the Christian Sunday for worship and personal renewal.

Hymn: "Glory and Praise to Our God" (*Gather, Second Edition*, 380)

Scripture Reading: Psalm 148:1-14

Comments:

1. In the Genesis account of creation, God spends six days working to make the world. On the seventh day the Lord rested. The purpose of the seventh day part of the story is to show us the importance of rest, relaxation and renewal.

2. The other message of the sabbath is that we should acknowledge that God is the author of all creation. This is the reason for weekly worship, our time of praise and thanks to God.

3. The Church imposed rest on Sunday so that people would be free to relax and worship God. Today we impose work on ourselves all the time. The rule of rest and prayer is more needed than ever.

The Result: The commercialism of Sunday and the overstress on work is dehumanizing.

What Should We Do?

A. Use the Sunday to pray and play.
B. Rediscover the joy of praising God.
C. Recover an awareness of God as creator and provider.

Resource: See the video "Babette's Feast" — a parable that illumines the meaning of Eucharist.

Strengthen Family Values — The Fourth Commandment

Goal: To motivate the students to struggle for the family values that create strong people and vital communities.

Hymn: "Love Divine, All Loves Excelling" (*Worship, Third Edition*, 588)

Scripture Reading: Luke 3:41-52

Comments:

1. The family is the domestic Church where the values of prayer, respect for one another and the best possibilities for human fulfillment take place. A family that fosters virtues and character will benefit the members and the society.

2. Parents and children must form a community with each other. While the parents must find ways to have loving discipline of their children, the children in turn should be caring, faithful and obedient to their parents.

3. In a society where the role of the father has been in decline, it must be revived and strengthened. Fatherless families, though they can work, are not the best way to go.

The Result: The collapse of the family in our culture is alarming and should be reversed.

What Should We Do?

A. Fathers must be promise keepers.
B. Parents should form support groups for better parenting.
C. The Church must be active in helping families succeed.

Resource: *The Things That Matter Most*, Cal Thomas, HarperCollins, NY, 1994.

Chapter 28

CHANGE THE CULTURE OF DEATH — AFFIRM LIFE: THE FIFTH COMMANDMENT

Goal: To become properly alarmed by the expansion of the culture of death, by upholding life's sacredness.

Hymn: "Lord of All Hopefulness" (*Breaking Bread* hymnal, 360)

Scripture Reading: Matthew 5:21-26; 38-48

Comments:

1. To the tragedy of abortion in our society is now added the possibility of euthanasia as evidenced by the introduction of assisted-suicide bills in many states. This comes as no surprise. If we can kill the weak unborn at the beginning of life, we will kill the weak elderly at the end of life.

2. In Holland euthanasia has moved from killing the terminally ill to killing the chronically ill, from killing those with physical afflictions to killing those with psychological illnesses, from killing those who want it to those who do not want it: There are one thousand terminations of life without request each year.

3. Replace the culture of death with the culture of life.

The Result: Life becomes cheap and coarse when we are willing to kill the weak.

What Should We Do?

A. Take up for life from conception to life's natural end.
B. Promote the sacredness and dignity of every human life.
C. Use political means to roll back abortion, euthanasia.

Resource: *The Gospel of Life* (*Evangelium Vitae*), Pope John Paul II, 1995.

Chapter 29

With This Ring, I Thee Wed . . . Forever — The Sixth Commandment

Goal: To retrieve the basic message of the sixth commandment about fidelity to the marriage vows.

Hymn: "Where True Love and Charity Are Found" (*Worship, Third Edition*, 598)

Scripture Reading: The Book of Tobit

Comments:

1. Our society has the highest divorce rate in the world. This imperils the stability of the family and the culture itself. We are engaged in a fatal experiment with family life that will have a tragic outcome for the whole culture.

2. The Church teaches that there should be an unbreakable bond between the unitive and procreative aspects of marriage. Bonding and babies go together.

3. When spouses fail to keep their most sacred promises, why should we expect anyone else to keep their promises? Adultery and fornication break both the natural law and God's eternal laws about the nature of marriage. When we break the commandments, the commandments break us.

The Result: Historically, cultures which have tried this decayed and died. Ours could too.

What Should We Do?

A. Support Marriage Encounter and Marriage Savers.
B. Renew commitment to the Church's teaching on marriage.
C. Pray daily for fidelity among spouses.

Resource: *Love and Responsibility*, Pope John Paul II, Farrar, Strauss, Giroux, NY, 1981.

Chapter 30

Don't Steal, Don't Treat People Unjustly — The Seventh Commandment

Goal: To see the connection between private property and the common good and the Church's social teachings.

Hymn: "The Cry of the Poor" (*Breaking Bread* hymnal, 581)

Scripture Reading: Amos 6:1-14

Comments:

1. In Genesis 1:28 and 2:15, God made human beings stewards of creation. We were given the earth as our property to develop it according to God's laws. Private property is a natural right. But its ownership must be exercised in relation to the universal destination of the goods of the earth, which is the common good.

2. The role of property is for the good of the family and the common good. One must be balanced by the other. Stealing is wrong because it takes from someone what is properly his. In justice we must see that everyone benefits from the goods of the earth.

3. The Church's social teachings begin with the dignity of the person and the family and their basic needs.

The Result: If there is no justice there will be social upheaval and war. Justice is the condition for peace.

What Should We Do?

A. Become familiar with the Church's social teachings.

B. Treat one another justly, mercifully, charitably.

C. Teach respect for property and the common good.

Resource: *Pastoral Constitution on the Church in the Modern World* (*Gaudium et Spes*), from the documents of the Second Vatican Council.

Chapter 31

Nothing but the Truth, the Whole Truth —
The Eighth Commandment

Goal: To recover a sense of the value of truth as the foundation of trust in a society.

Hymn: "How Firm a Foundation" (*Breaking Bread* hymnal, 344)

Scripture Reading: I John 1:5-10

Comments:

1. It has been said that lying is as American as apple pie. That's too bad, because the collapse of truth-telling leads to the erosion of trust in one another. If I can't believe what you say, then I will not trust you ever again.

2. Jesus made it clear that he was a witness to the truth. He even went so far as to say, "I am the truth." We could not see light in Jesus' teachings if they were not true. Truth is light. Lies are darkness.

3. The decline of truth-telling is related to relativism, which claims there is no truth, only opinion. The loss of confidence in knowing truth removes fear of lying.

The Result: The common sense expectation that people can be trusted to tell the truth is threatened by deceit.

What Should We Do?

A. Tell the truth, the whole truth, all the time.
B. Build trust in our communities with truth.
C. Regain confidence that truth can be known.

Resource: *People of the Lie*, M. Scott Peck, Touchstone, NY, 1983.

Chapter 32

BLESSED ARE THE PURE IN HEART — THE NINTH COMMANDMENT

Goal: To complement the teaching of the sixth commandment on sex and marriage with the teaching of chastity.

Hymn: "Jesus Shall Reign" (*Worship, Third Edition*, 492)

Scripture Reading: Daniel 13:1-63

Comments:

1. If the body is going to be pure, then the soul must be chaste. Jesus said that happiness accompanies being "pure of heart." A chaste mind and heart leads to a pure body.

2. The capital sin of lust is opposed to purity of heart. Jesus said that adultery is wrong. But lust in the heart is wrong as well because it leads to adultery of the body.

3. The commercialization of lust in our culture presents everyone with daily temptations to become lustful. It is a small wonder the society is filled with rapes, sexual abuse, fornication and adultery and homosexual behavior. Ideas have consequences. So do lustful thoughts and feelings.

The Result: The rise of immoral sexual behavior has led to unwanted pregnancies, sexual abuse and broken marriages.

What Should We Do?

A. Counter lust with the cultivation of a chaste mind.
B. Use prayer, common sense and discipline to be chaste.
C. Treat people as persons of dignity, not sex objects.

Resource: *Humanae Vitae, Making Healthier Happier People*, 4 audiocassettes, Janet Smith, St. Joseph Communications, 800/526-2151.

Chapter 33

Greed Vs. Generosity —
The Tenth Commandment

Goal: To see that the capital sin of greed, which is the love of money, is the root of all evil.

Hymn: "Here I Am, Lord" (*Gather, Second Edition*, 492)

Scripture Reading: I Timothy 6:3-10

Comments:

1. The letter to Timothy teaches that the love of money is the root of all evil. Virtually all wars have economic injustice behind them, cases where greedy nations want more land, more money, simply more of every material gain.

2. Greed consumes the passions of those who give into it. Things don't just stop with money, but branch out into extreme sex, power and other dehumanizing attitudes.

3. Greed is one of the greatest causes of poverty because the avaricious do not use money productively for the good of others, but rather selfishly for their own gratification.

The Result: It is no secret that most wars and economic depressions can be traced to greed.

What Should We Do?

A. Practice detachment and poverty of spirit.
B. Learn the joy of giving.
C. Replace greed with generosity.

Resource: *The Moral Sense*, James Q. Wilson, Free Press (Macmillan), NY, 1993.

Chapter 34

PRAYER: BREAD FOR OUR FAITH JOURNEY

Goal: To acquire a desire for prayer and the habit of praying always.

Hymn: "Father, We Thank Thee, Who Hast Planted" (*Worship, Third Edition*, 558)

Scripture Reading: Psalm 150:1-6

Comments:

1. Prayer is loving communion with God. Prayer is the lifting up of our minds, hearts and bodies to God with the hope of having a deeper relationship with the Lord. Prayer is a friendly conversation with Jesus.

2. Prayer is the soul of faith, the spirit of the liturgy, the reason why we can be moral. Without prayer we take the breath out of religion, with a result that faith dries up.

3. Prayer includes meditation, contemplation, vocal prayer, liturgical worship, hymn singing and other forms of communing with God. The greatest prayer is the Our Father. The Bible devotes thousands of passages to prayer.

The Result: Whenever a diocese or parish or family is prayerful, great graces flow upon the participants.

What Should We Do?

A. Pray always (I Thessalonians 5:17) .
B. Pray with others at liturgy, in homes and elsewhere.
C. Learn how to pray in silence, the prayer of the heart.

Resource: *Modern Spiritual Writers*, Charles Healey, SJ, Alba House, NY, 1989.

Chapter 35

THE SEVEN PETITIONS OF THE OUR FATHER

Goal: To appreciate the greatest of all prayers, the Our Father, taught to us by Jesus himself.

Hymn: The "Our Father" (Chant, from the Mass)

Scripture Reading: Luke 11:1-4

Comments:

1. The Our Father has so attracted many of the saints that they have written commentaries on it. Augustine wrote seven commentaries on the Our Father. Other famous works include that of Teresa of Ávila.

2. The seven petitions of the Our Father outline the basics of all prayer. By turning attention to the Father, Jesus reminds us that prayer begins with focusing on God. By asking us to say "our," Jesus associates us with his own divine filiation.

3. The various petitions deserve from us a lifetime of reflection, especially the ones about daily bread, including Eucharist, and forgiveness, a gift for ourselves and others.

The Result: Of the thousands of books written on prayer, the fifty-three words of the Our Father tell us all about it in a simple, direct way.

What Should We Do?

A. Pray the Our Father slowly, thinking of each petition.
B. Pick the petition you need most right now.
C. Use your special petition for meditative prayer.

Resource: *Enfolded in Love*, Julian of Norwich, Darton, London, 1993.

Chapter 36

O Blest Communion, Fellowship Divine:
The Communion of Saints

Goal: To awaken in ourselves an awareness of the existence of the Communion of Saints in heaven, earth and purgatory.

Hymn: "For All the Saints" (*Worship, Third Edition*, 705)

Scripture Reading: Revelation 8:9-17

Comments:

1. The Communion of Saints means that some of Christ's disciples are pilgrims on earth; others have died and are in purgatory, being purified; still others are in glory contemplating God himself.

2. On earth the members of the Church pray together, show one another love and bear one another's burdens. We pray to God for each other's intentions. We also pray for the souls in purgatory. We ask Mary and the saints in heaven to pray for us.

3. Thus the Communion of Saints is a community of all disciples of Jesus; those on earth and in purgatory are helped by those in heaven.

The Result: The Communion of Saints exemplifies the love of Jesus in a most effective manner.

What Should We Do?

A. Practice Communion of Saints awareness.
B. Pray for the souls in purgatory.
C. Ask Mary, the angels and saints to pray for us.

Resource: *Lives of the Saints You Should Know*, Margaret and Matthew Bunson, Our Sunday Visitor, Huntington, IN, 1994.

Epilogue

"The Church has widely shared in concern about how to impart catechesis to children and young people. God grant that the attention thus aroused will long endure in the Church's consciousness. In this way the Synod has been valuable for the whole Church by seeking to trace with the greatest possible precision the complex characteristics of present-day youth; by showing that these young persons speak a language into which the message of Jesus must be translated with patience and wisdom and without betrayal; by demonstrating that, in spite of appearances, these young people have within them, even though often in a confused way, not just a readiness or openness, but rather a desire to know 'Jesus . . . who is called Christ' (Mt 1:16); and by indicating that if the work of catechesis is to be carried out rigorously and seriously, it is today more difficult and tiring than ever before, because of the obstacles that it meets; but it is also more consoling, because of the depth of the response it receives from children and young people. This is a treasure the Church can and should count on in the years ahead."

(On Catechesis in Our Time, Catechesi Tradendae, 40, John Paul II, 1979)

Hymnal Publishers

Worship, Third Edition, © 1986 by G.I.A. Publications, Inc., 7404 South Mason Avenue, Chicago, Illinois 60638.

Gather, Second Edition, © 1994 by G.I.A. Publications, Inc., 7404 South Mason Avenue, Chicago, Illinois 60638.

Gather, © 1988 by G.I.A. Publications, Inc., 7404 South Mason Avenue, Chicago, Illinois 60638.

Breaking Bread, Bari Colombari, Editor, Oregon Catholic Press, 5536 NE Hassalo, Portland, Oregon 97213.